P9-DGI-320

Learning to Read, Step by Step!

Ready to Read **Preschool–Kindergarten**
• big type and easy words • rhyme and rhythm • picture clues
For children who know the alphabet and are eager to begin reading.

Reading with Help **Preschool–Grade 1**
• basic vocabulary • short sentences • simple stories
For children who recognize familiar words and sound out new words with help.

Reading on Your Own **Grades 1–3**
• engaging characters • easy-to-follow plots • popular topics
For children who are ready to read on their own.

Reading Paragraphs **Grades 2–3**
• challenging vocabulary • short paragraphs • exciting stories
For newly independent readers who read simple sentences with confidence.

Ready for Chapters **Grades 2–4**
• chapters • longer paragraphs • full-color art
For children who want to take the plunge into chapter books but still like colorful pictures.

STEP INTO READING® is designed to give every child a successful reading experience. The grade levels are only guides; children will progress through the steps at their own speed, developing confidence in their reading. The F&P Text Level on the back cover serves as another tool to help you choose the right book for your child.

Remember, a lifetime love of reading starts with a single step!

For David—slow, but steady! —B.B.

Text copyright © 2016 by Bonnie Bader

All rights reserved. Published in the United States by Random House Children's Books, a division of Penguin Random House LLC, New York. Originally published in hardcover in the United States by Penguin Young Readers, an imprint of Penguin Random House LLC, New York, in 2016.

Step into Reading, Random House, and the Random House colophon are registered trademarks of Penguin Random House LLC.

Photograph credits: cover: baby sloth © Thinkstock/Snic320, climbing sloth © Thinkstock/Eric Isselée; pages 3, 15: © Getty Images/Hoberman Collection; page 4: © Thinkstock/JonathanNicholls; page 5: © Thinkstock/SivelstreSelva; pages 1, 6–7: © Thinkstock/Eric Isselée; page 8: © Thinkstock/ctrlaplus1; page 9: © Thinkstock/miroslav_1; page 10: © Thinkstock/Julio Viard; page 11: © Thinkstock/JackF; page 12: © Thinkstock/Eric Isselée; page 13: © Thinkstock/webguzs; page 14: © Thinkstock/JackKa; page 16: © Thinkstock/Jozev; page 17: © Getty Images/Wolfgang Kaehler; page 18: © Getty Images/Hoberman Collection; page 19: © Corbis; page 20: © Thinkstock/Eric Middelkoop; page 21: © Getty Images/DEA/C. DANI I. JESKE; pages 22–23: © Thinkstock/Seubsai; page 24: ants © Thinkstock/onlyyouqj, grasshopper © Thinkstock/Andreas Argirakis, lizard © Thinkstock/ananaline, mosquito © Thinkstock/JoyTasa; page 25: © Corbis/Suzi Eszterhas; page 26: © Getty Images/RODRIGO ARANGUA; page 27: © Corbis/Piotr Naskrecki; page 28: © Corbis/James Christensen; page 29: © Corbis/Wayne Lynch; page 30: © Getty Images/RODRIGO ARANGUA; page 31: © Thinkstock/Adam_C_King; page 32: © Thinkstock/tane-mahuta.

Visit us on the Web!
StepIntoReading.com
rhcbooks.com

Educators and librarians, for a variety of teaching tools, visit us at
RHTeachersLibrarians.com

Library of Congress Cataloging-in-Publication Data is available upon request.
ISBN 978-0-593-43244-0 (trade) — ISBN 978-0-593-43245-7 (lib. bdg.)

Printed in the United States of America
10 9 8 7 6 5 4 3 2 1

This book has been officially leveled by using the F&P Text Level Gradient™ Leveling System.

Random House Children's Books supports the First Amendment and celebrates the right to read.

Penguin Random House LLC supports copyright. Copyright fuels creativity, encourages diverse voices, promotes free speech, and creates a vibrant culture. Thank you for buying an authorized edition of this book and for complying with copyright laws by not reproducing, scanning, or distributing any part in any form without permission. You are supporting writers and allowing Penguin Random House to publish books for every reader.

STEP 2
READING WITH HELP
STEP INTO READING®
A SCIENCE READER
SLOW, SLOW SLOTHS
by Bonnie Bader
Random House New York

Slow,

slow

sloths!

Sloths are mammals. They live in the rain forests of Central and South America.

Sloths have long arms
and long fur.
Are they in the
same family
as monkeys?

No!

Sloths are in the same family

as armadillos.

And anteaters.

There are two types of sloths.

The two-toed sloth has two claws

on its front feet.

The three-toed sloth has three claws on its front feet.

All sloths have round heads.

And three- to four-inch claws.

And little ears.

And short tails.

And sad-looking eyes.

But the three-toed sloth

looks like it is always smiling!

Sloths are born high up
in the trees.
Baby sloths cling to
their mothers' bellies
until they can take care
of themselves.

A young sloth likes to stay close
to its mother.
It can live with her
for up to four years.

Now it is all grown up.

It is about two feet long.

It weighs between 8 and 17 pounds.

Sloths like to live
by themselves.

They sleep a lot.
Sloths sleep between
15 and 20 hours a day.

Two-toed sloths

are awake at night.

Sloths hook their claws onto tree branches. They hang upside down by their long arms.

Sloths sleep and sleep and sleep.

Sloths don't eat much.

They sometimes eat small insects.

Or small lizards.

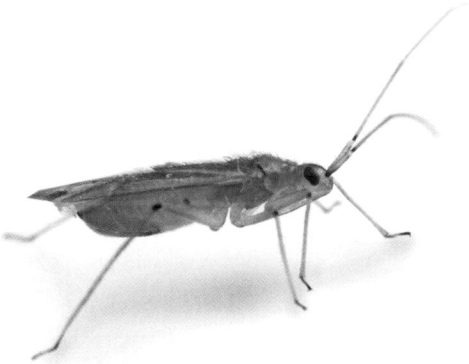

But they mostly eat leaves.

Leaves do not give them

much energy.

This is one reason sloths are

so slow!

The sloth's long claws make it

hard to walk on the ground.

So it stays in the trees.

Some sloths stay in the same tree for years.

The only time they come down is to go to the bathroom.

Or to go for a swim.

Plop! The sloth falls from the tree

into the river.

Sloths are great swimmers.

Sloths move so slowly that algae (say: AL-gee) grows on their fur. This green plant helps sloths hide from their enemies.

But they can't always hide.

Here comes a harpy eagle!

Swipe! The sloth bats at

the harpy eagle with

its long, sharp claws.

The sloth hisses.

It lets out a loud yell.

The harpy eagle flies away.

The sloth is tired

from fighting off its enemy.

It slowly climbs up the tree

and goes to sleep.

Sleep tight, slow, slow sloth!